THE AGILE REVOLUTION

A GUIDE FOR BUSINESS ON AGILE WORKING

Copyright © 2017 BPS World and Onyx Media and Communications

Permission granted to reproduce for personal and educational use only. Commercial copying, hiring, lending is prohibited.

RESEARCHED AND PRODUCED BY:

Contents

Introduction	7
Chapter 1	8
What's the appeal, definition and the history?	8
What's the appeal?	9
Better diversity and access	9
Environmentally friendly	10
A return to communities	10
More suited to millennials	11
What does it look like?	11
What agile working practices can a company offer?	11
Agile working v. flexible working	12
Case Study: Birmingham City Council	12
Case Study: Lloyds Banking Group	13
The history of work	13
Chapter 2	15
The practical implications of agile working	15
Sector	15
Culture	16
The Office	18
What goes wrong?	20
Chapter 3	22
What is the social impact	22
Commuting time and cost	22
Exclusion of disabled people	22
Exclusion of those with caring responsibilities	23
Exclusion of our most experienced	23
Destruction of local communities	24

Distortion of housing costs	25
Employment rights	25
Fair and available for all?	26
Chapter 4	28
What is the business impact?	28
Thinking global	28
Agile as a business model	29
An investor's viewpoint	29
Skills	29
Diversity	30
Chapter 5	32
How to create an agile workforce	32
Shifting perceptions	32
Restructuring workloads	33
Employees working for others	33
Technology	34
Meetings and teamwork	35
Training	35
Top tips from Megan Knapp, start-up coach & business strategist:	36
Case Study: The CAB Studios approach	36
Testing the water	37
Chapter 6	38
How do you measure its impact?	38
Productivity	38
Case study – Ctrip in China	39
Costs	40
Recruitment	41
Customers	42
Chapter 7	43
What is the future of agile working?	43
Recruitment	44
The Office	44
Housing	45

    Infrastructure   45

    Public Policy   46

    The Global Picture   46

    A Final Word   48

Authors and Contributors   50

Introduction

Agile working is a growing trend. It does not suit all businesses but all should understand it if they want to remain competitive. This book provides a guide to employers. It outlines the practical implications involved as well as the overall business benefits. It also takes a frank look at where it's not suitable.

Desk research is complemented by new quantitative and qualitative research with contributions from experts, economists, futurologists and leading business thinkers who have experienced agile working. We are grateful to all our contributors.

The research answers questions such as:

What is agile working? - Agile working is often confused with flexible working and remote working. What is the authoritative definition and what is its history? Is it really a new concept? What is its appeal?

What are the practical implications? - Agile working suits some people and some organisations, and parts of organisations, and not others. What do you need to think about before you even start to consider an agile working policy?

What is the social impact? – Successful businesses take corporate social responsibility (CSR) very seriously. It is a major influencing factor in winning customers and recruiting and retaining the best people. What is the impact of traditional working practices on society and how will a move to agile working help?

What is the business impact? – What is the impact of agile working on productivity and things such as skills shortages? What will your customers think? Why have some companies returned to traditional working?

How do you create an agile workforce? - How do you move towards agile working? What are the lessons from those who have already done it?

How do you measure its impact? - How can you tell if your agile working policy is delivering bottom-line business benefits, what do you measure?

What does the future look like? - According to leading futurologists and studies, the rise of agile working will have far more impact than politicians or business leaders realise. What are their predictions?

Chapter 1
What's the appeal, definition and the history?

In February 2001, a group of IT consultants met at a ski resort in Utah to discuss how they could uncover better ways of developing software. One of the biggest problems they all faced was the imposition of documentation driven, heavyweight processes through corporate power structures.[1]

After two days of debate, they called themselves *The Agile Alliance* and agreed on the following set of values:

> Individuals and interactions over processes and tools
> Working software over comprehensive documentation
> Customer collaboration over contract negotiation
> Responding to change over following a plan

Jim Highsmith, one of the attendees that weekend, summarised the reasoning behind this alliance for an online manifesto, in which he pointed out that their ultimate aim was to improve a world that had become dominated by companies with arcane policies and Dilbert[2] manifestations of 'make-work':

"The Agile movement is not anti-methodology, in fact, many of us want to restore credibility to the word methodology," he wrote. "We want to restore a balance. We embrace modelling, but not in order to file some diagram in a dusty corporate repository. We embrace documentation, but not hundreds of pages of never-maintained and rarely-used tomes. We plan, but recognise the limits of planning in a turbulent environment."

The agile software development movement has now become the de facto way of developing software in all businesses (not just start-ups). This is because timescales for change are impossible to meet using traditional code development, testing and deployment techniques.

However, this book is not focussed on just the Agile Movement, but on the much wider revolution that is breaking down the structures around work as we know them. Advances in technology have resulted in most of us working from home some of the time, even if that is just outside office hours to catch up. This has led many to question how important it is for us to attend an office every day to work. If we are being asked to be agile when we're "off duty", to answer emails in the evening and to check things at weekends, shouldn't the change go both ways?

Technology has also changed the nature of work. Léon Benjamin, a co-founder of Sei Mani, with 25 years' experience delivering transformation programmes to major global brands explained; "We need to deal with the reality that the unit of work is no longer necessarily a whole job. Automation, AI and other mega trends affecting the nature of work are here now.

---

[1] The Agile Manifesto http://agilemanifesto.org/history.html
[2] Wikipedia https://en.wikipedia.org/wiki/Dilbert_principle

What's the appeal?

The internet and smartphones have changed the way we are able to manage our lives. At the same time, we are faced with social and economic challenges that make us question how we live and work. Agile working offers a solution to many of these challenges and both the young and old are embracing it.

William Higham, futurologist and founder of NextBigThing explained why he thinks the trend for agile working is taking off so quickly, when flexible working took decades to become accepted (and in many organisations still isn't, despite legislation):

"The majority of Britons are wandering around with their mobile phones at weekends, they might be sending emails, looking up their local cinema to see what films they could watch on a Saturday night, or they could be shopping from the comfort of their sofa. Everything they do is mobile and has no time constraint.

"Come Monday morning, they go into their place of work to be greeted by a fixed computer, a fixed phone, and fixed hierarchy. This doesn't make sense when we no longer live in a fixed world. The traditional workplace set-up isn't aligned with the way we live our lives; we are used to living agile so working that way comes naturally."

As a result, increasing numbers of workers are frustrated by corporate life and are keen to find an alternative to these standard "fixed" routines. Faced with crowded commutes and cities, they lack motivation and want something else. The Stoddard Review: The Workplace Advantage[3] found that only 53% of workers think their workplace allows them to work productively.

The notion that the office may not be the best place to work would have seemed absurd at the turn of the last century, when home working was considered a difficult to manage perk for mothers. Yet 17 years in, most of us now question it. This change in attitude has seen a rising trend in people finding alternative places to work, whether that's from home, in work hubs or in coffee shops. One recent study[4] showed that 81% of office workers now spend three and a half hours there each week. And while it was once seen as the preserve of start-ups, the same study found that three out of four staff working for companies with over 250 employees prefer working from a coffee shop.

The statistics tell their own story: 50% of millennials, 40% of Gen X and 35% of boomers say burnout is motivating them to consider changing jobs and 53% of millennials say a healthy work-life balance would make them stay at their job [5]

It is not just technology and personal preference that has driven this trend, there are also a number of social reasons why agile working has become popular. These are outlined below and then explored in more detail later in this book.

---

[3] The Stoddard Review – The Work Place Advantage Published in May 2016 http://stoddartreview.com/
[4] MyVoucher Code 2017
[5] Life Coach https://www.lifecoachmarcia.com/

Better diversity and access

The diversity and access issue has driven demand for flexible working, which has led to agile working.

Women have traditionally taken on the role of carers, for children, the elderly and the disabled. However, ONS figures for 2016 showed that 69.1% of women (aged 16-64) are now in work. Changing attitudes mean that women are now more likely to be judged for not being in work and for many families the income is an economic necessity, so even though the challenges of caring and working are extremely difficult to manage, these carers will continue to be an important part of the work force.

It helps if carers can work part-time. Government data for the first three months of 2017 showed that there were 8.52 million people working part-time, 10,000 more than for a year earlier.[6] Responsibilities are also made more challenging for carers if they can't get home quickly when needed, and a typical commuter will find it a challenge to get home in time to collect a child from nursery.

For people with disabilities, technology can enable them to be economically active when previously their lack of mobility, for example, would have made it impossible for them to work. Yet without agile working these people are still needlessly stuck at home, reliant on the state.

Older workers are now more likely to stay in the workforce for longer; they're healthier for longer and reject the old ideas about who and what a 60-plus person should be. As high-profile people like The Rolling Stones grow old disgracefully, people reject the notion of retirement, but neither do they want to be tied to a desk five days a week from nine to five. They want to work and feel valued, but also have a life outside work.

Environmentally friendly

We have accepted overcrowded cities, air pollution and transport congestion as a fact of modern life, but those who have embraced agile working question that. Without the demand from employers for us all to be at a set place, at a set time, the environment would see a radical change for the better.

In the past, air pollution, in industrialising countries, was caused by the burning of fossil fuels (both domestically and industrially). However, in most cases, this has been steadily improving over the years. The main cause of air pollution world-wide is now traffic[7].

The pollutants caused by traffic have a major impact on human health, welfare and the environment. Yet the annual safe limits set by government are being regularly breached. In London, for example, annual air pollution limit for the whole of 2017 was exceeded in the first five days of the year. Yet the World Health Organisation, which gathers average particulate levels from cities around the world, believes that air pollution in Bejing is five times worse than in London.

---

[6] Office of National Statistics UK Labour Market report https://www.ons.gov.uk/employmentandlabourmarket
[7] Department for Environment Food and Rural Affairs https://uk-air.defra.gov.uk/air-pollution/causes

A return to communities

Do you know your next-door neighbour? A poll in 2013 for Churchill Insurance[8] found that over a third of people would not even recognise their neighbour if they saw them. This breakdown of communities is most common in places where most people commute to work; the so-called dormitory towns. It means that we have lost the community spirit that has been shown to be so beneficial to mental health and well-being.

More suited to millennials

Millennials have challenged the traditional ways of working and Generation Z are expected to flat out reject them. These generations are more entrepreneurial in their attitudes and some millennials have started successful high-profile businesses that prove that new ways of working can be highly profitable. They have grown up with technology, so instinctively will make it work for them. They demand opportunities to develop their skills, they're more aware and concerned about the environment, they expect the culture they work in to promote equality and they aim to make the world a better place. A 2015 report by Sparks and Honey [9] found that 80% of millennials were aware of the impact humans have on the planet and 26% of 16 to 19 year olds were volunteering.

According to Simon Conington, Managing Director and Founder of BPS World, millennials are also less likely to remain in one place: "What employees now want from their working lives has been changing radically, with millennials seeking contract careers that turn established attitudes on their heads. Nearly half of employees now believe a job for life will soon be a thing of the past and that people will increasingly work independently, rather than for large organisations."[10]

What does it look like?

The above issues are covered in more detail in later chapters. Agile working offers a solution to all of them by breaking down the old walls and creating new ways of working such as flexible hours, zero-hour contracts, freelance assignments and remote logins, based on four dimensions:

- Time (when do people work?)
- Location (where do people work?)
- Role (what do people do?)
- Source (who carries out the work?)[11]

"Imagine organisations in which most workers aren't employees at all, but electronically connected freelancers living wherever they want to. And imagine that all this freedom in business lets people get more of whatever they really want in life; money, interesting work, the chance to help others, or time with their families." Thomas Malone, The Future of Work.

---

[8] https://www.churchill.com/press-office/releases/2013/do-you-know-your-neighbours-name
[9] https://www.slideshare.net/sparksandhoney/generation-z-final-june-17
[10] Total Immersion – White Paper published by BPS World
[11] The Agile Future Forum http://www.agile.org.uk/what-is-agile-working/

What agile working practices can a company offer?

- Flexible working - this gives employees greater freedom to create a work/life balance and thus keeps them happier and more loyal to the brand
- Part-time opportunities - this retains qualified staff for half the cost of full-time employees while increasing productivity
- Job shares - this essentially brings you the expertise of two people for the price of one
- Freelance work - this can be a good way for companies to manage money by adapting their size to their work flow and gives people the freedom to work elsewhere

But to be truly agile in its working practices the company should also consider:

- Allowing employees to take other work with other employers (if it doesn't cause a conflict of interest)
- Being goal-focussed rather than hours-focussed (to measure what is achieved instead of how many hours someone put in)
- To allow employees to choose their place of work

According to Paul Allsopp, managing director of The Agile Organisation, agile working is "about bringing people, processes, connectivity and technology, time and place together to find the most appropriate and effective way of working to carry out a particular task. It is working within guidelines (of the task) but without boundaries (of how you achieve it)."

This definition has been extensively used by other organisations in publications and glossaries, including NHS England, the Science Council and the Employers Network for Equality and Inclusion. However, it is hard to pin down an exact definition of agile working due to its very essence of being open to interpretation within each organisation. In the end, it comes down to whatever will create a more balanced, motivated, innovative and productive team. It involves maximum flexibility, minimum constraints and a willingness to constantly evolve to suit the ever-changing needs of both the business and employees.

Agile working v. flexible working

People often confuse agile working with flexible working. In a Financial Times article,[12] journalist Alison Maitland explained flexible working arrangements as "individually negotiated, require management permission and are seen primarily as an employee benefit and an exception to the norm." By contrast, agile working arrangements are "business-driven, harnessing technology to create a new norm where everyone may work anytime, anywhere, provided business needs are met… It requires a change from management by inputs (time and presence) to management by outcomes."

---

[12] Financial Times https://www.ft.com/content/c2ba1250-36de-11e6-a780-b48ed7b6126f

Case Study: Birmingham City Council

In 2006, Birmingham City Council (BCC), England's largest local authority with over 1 million customers, modernised their back-office culture and buildings in order to transform the way they delivered their services. This included moving 78 offices into eight, which saved £100m, and creating optimal locations for 10,000 employees, such as the opportunity to do extra hours from home in the evenings.[13]

According to Peter Jones, director of property at BCC, the work done amounts to one of the most significant change programmes undertaken by any public-sector organisation since the advent of Local Government reform in 1972. "If all Local Authorities achieved the same as us, together we would save £3 billion of cashable benefits over 25 years," he said in the final report.

Case Study: Lloyds Banking Group

Agile working is at the heart of Lloyd's Banking Group's strategy. In 2015, the company improved its job share register and launched an enhanced Shared Parental policy to offer greater choice and flexibility for its working parents. The following year, it launched a new colleague network called Family Matters, which holds events covering topics from caring for children/adults and managing a career to regular overviews of the Group's Paternity policy. Over the next three years, the banking group plans to invest £1 billion in its digital offering to ensure it has a strong technology infrastructure for agile working to be embedded in the business.[14]

The history of work

Many people see agile working as highly innovative or dangerously experimental. How will employees react when the traditional working practices, proved over generations to work, are changed in favour of something untried? The irony is businesses are in fact coming full circle, as agile working is nothing new. People used a similar approach in the earliest stages of human civilization, when work was confined to simple tasks involving basic human needs: food, child care, shelter. The division of labour began when individuals showed proficiency in certain tasks, which then developed from foraging and hunting to pottery, textiles and agriculture.[15] But even then, work tended to be seasonal and not tied to one place; it happened all around you. 18th century manufacturing of textiles was often done in people's homes using basic tools and machines, for example, hence the term 'cottage industry'. And the payoff was tied to the output, not the number of hours put in. As Higham explained: "'work' was all about results and what you produced."

The first purpose-built office block was created in 1729. It was situated in the City, on Leadenhall Street and housed the East India Company, whose long-distance trading was creating a lot of paperwork.

---

[13] BCC http://www.telerealtrillium.com/cms/cms_files/bcc_booklet_soft_copy_(2).pdf
[14] Lloyds http://www.lloydsbankinggroup.com/our-group/responsible-business/inclusion-and-diversity/agile-working/
[15] Britannica https://www.britannica.com/topic/history-of-work-organization-648000

Charles Lamb, a clerk who started work there at the age of 17 wrote: "On Friday I was at the office from 10 in the morning (two hours dinner except) to 11 at night - last night till 9."

By the mid-18th century, population growth and rising foreign trade increased demand for manufacturing goods and so more offices were built, as well as factories. The first factory was built in 1769 near Derby and employed 800 people by 1789.

The factories in particular took rigid processes to the extreme, forcing people to sign in and out, work 12-hour days in poor conditions and for little pay. In 1817, the holiday allowance of £10 a year was cut for new members of staff and Saturday became a full working day. They also made work in the fields redundant, which lead to severe unemployment, poverty and overcrowding as people started to migrate from the country to the city in search of work.[16]

By the early 1900s, the idea that managers could improve workplace efficiency really took hold. This led to the first open plan office in 1906, followed by the rise of the cubicle once managers realised too much supervision stifled productivity. Their strong, domineering presence remained however until the 1990s when the rise of hot-desking and the office hotel fuelled the trend towards greater employee autonomy - a precursor to agile working.

Even the use of the coffee house as a workplace harks back to history. Author Steve Johnson explained in a 2010 TED talk that before coffee houses in the 17th Century, people would not risk drinking water without using alcohol as an antibacterial agent, so drunkenness was common. "It's not an accident that a great flowering of innovation happened as England switched to tea and coffee," which made them sharper and more alert; "But the architecture of the space was just as important. It was where people would get together from different backgrounds, "It was a space where ideas could have sex. This was their conjugal bed, in a sense. And an astonishing number of innovations from this period have a coffee house somewhere in their story."

---

[16] BBC   http://www.bbc.co.uk/news/magazine-23372401

Chapter 2
The practical implications of agile working

With the benefits becoming clearer, the trend for agile working is finally taking off. According to Scott Steedman, director of standards at the BSI (British Standards Institute) Group, in the competitive business environment, more and more organisations are realising the importance of unlocking their full potential, he explained; "Employing effective practices is a key goal for all businesses… regardless of size or sector".

However, there are some challenges you need to consider before you can plan an agile working policy for all or part of your business. These will vary according to the sector you're in, how accepted and embedded new ways of working already are, whether you're large or small, start-up or established and the nature of the work you're doing.

Sector

IT, communications and creative businesses have been quick to make changes because innovation is a fundamental part of what they do. They also tend to have a younger workforce who are naturally more agile in the way they work. Facebook, for example, encourages staff to live near the company headquarters through a US$10,000 bonus scheme and allows them to work from home on Wednesdays.

However not all industries are finding it so easy. Transport, hospitality, retail and education for example, rely heavily upon people being physically present to get the work done. Amanda Underwood, Group HR Director at WSH, the parent company for well-known restaurant brands including Benugo and Searcy's, explains the challenge for the hospitality industry: "Any business where you are serving a customer, and you promise to open and close at a certain time, requires certainty that people will be there to respond to that customer need. This does limit options when it comes to agile working, but it doesn't mean that hospitality businesses should be completely lacking in flexibility either. The fact that staff at restaurants, bars and hotels are mostly shift workers means there are ways they can make their hours work around them, by choosing shifts to suit, and sometimes asking to swap or change if a new commitment arises. This isn't entirely 'agile' but offering some degree of flexibility certainly helps with employee retention and engagement, without impacting the customer."

Underwood believes retail, travel, telecoms and property may also face challenges in adopting agile working, but for slightly different reasons. "These tend to be business with tight margins, with significant investment in assets or a physical product. Because of this, what they would need to spend on technology, or on adapting their workspace for agile working, is often seen as a deterrent; they are worried about the upfront cost and feel uncertain about the actual benefits it delivers."

Size
Larger companies struggle to introduce business-wide changes at speed due to the breadth of what they do. Companies employing up to 10 people are significantly more likely to offer flexible working

opportunities to their staff, for example, than their mid-sized (11-150 employees) or large (251+ employees) counterparts.[17]

"Imposing an organisation-wide agile working policy all at once on a larger company, is very ill advised," says Kirstie Kelly, Executive HR Director at CAB Studios and Head of Diversity and Inclusion at Capita. "Businesses need to consider how it will land at a divisional level, consider how to support employees through the transition, what processes need to be in place etc.

"Capita is a good example. Could they drive out an agile working policy for an IT development team with offshore customers and apply the same policy for a contingent workforce that are supporting security at a large-scale event? Of course not! They would need to consider it at divisional level and implement it in a way that is fit for purpose for each unit of the business."

Underwood agrees that a forced, organisation-wide roll out of agile working would be almost destined to fail, but says that trialling it in 'pockets' of the business and ensuring that successes are widely documented and talked about can help get more widespread buy-in: "If a manager trials agile working, and as a result their team are happier, productive and enthusiastic, then another manager is going to be more intrigued and open to the idea, wanting a bit of that enthusiasm and productivity for their own team. It's encouraging healthy competition, but this would only work if the culture is one of openness and there's a willingness to drive change, even on a small scale."

Politics

Figures from the House of Commons Women and Equalities Committee[18] show that the public and voluntary sectors are leading the way in embracing the trend for agile working. 86% of employers in the public sector offer part-time working, 69% offer job shares and 65% offer flexi-time. In the voluntary sector, 84% of firms offer part-time work, 69% job shares and 56% flexi-time.

However, according to Eve Poole, lecturer at Ashridge Business School, there are political sensitivities: "The public sector is financed by the public purse, so accountability is just the cost of doing business. This has traditionally been delivered through detailed contracts and documentation, so that every stage of the process bears scrutiny. Prioritising outcome over process does not come easily to those schooled in this discipline."

Culture

Company culture is a huge driving force in people deciding whether or not to work for an organisation.

BPS World's White Paper, Total Immersion[19], found that culture was more important than salary. Although the evidence is that offering agile working will make it easier for an organisation to attract the right people, there is a danger that if you change company culture too quickly and too radically some staff will leave.

---

[17] RSA https://www.thersa.org/discover/publications-and-articles/reports/the-flex-factor
[18] https://publications.parliament.uk/pa/cm201516/cmselect/cmwomeq/584/584.pdf
[19] Total Immersion - Available free to download from www.bps_world.com - Published October 2014

Of course, this isn't an excuse not to introduce agile working at all, as you may struggle to recruit and retain good employees if you don't move towards agile working. But you do need to take it a step at a time. If, for example, you have a workforce that is used to working nine to five in an office, it makes sense to gradually move to agile working through flexible working and options to work from home and not to assume everyone will embrace it. People need to be given a choice (where practical).

As Higham explained: "Some people believe working remotely is a negative as they want to work with others or find it very difficult to work alone. I would argue that there are people who don't want to go into an office *every day* for various reasons but they like the social aspect of it. There are also plenty of people who currently work from home the majority of the time, and they will admit to feelings of loneliness or that they crave the ability to bounce ideas off others and work collaboratively."

So, be warned, this way of working does not suit everyone. Many also prefer to be judged on presenteeism and would worry if they had to prove their value to a team in terms of outcomes. There is nowhere to hide and even good, but less confident, employees will find that a daunting prospect. It can also create tension within the team. When you're measured solely on output, someone blocking you delivering on a goal can feel personal. Some team members may also become more fixated on delivering their own goals, to the detriment of the bigger picture, and some will feel that your office is very much part of the package they signed up to when they joined your organisation.

Anne Cantelo explained what happened at Onyx, a business communications consultancy based in London. "We had an expensive, but lovely, office in London's Soho. The lease was up for renewal and the landlord put the rent up significantly which made it unaffordable, and we had little time to find a new office, so we moved to become a fully agile business. We already offered part-time working, flexible working and home working so I didn't think this was going to be too much of a change, but the young team at the time actively pushed to go back to working in an office. They wanted the buzz and social credibility of working in Soho, it was one of the reasons they joined Onyx, so I found somewhere for occasional use but the younger team members still left. We now have a much more senior team, spread out across the UK, so it hasn't been bad for Onyx, but it taught me that you can't assume that everyone wants to embrace agile working, you have to be prepared for the fact that some don't want it."

People have different working styles. One size won't fit all and a key benefit of agile working is that it should mean that your employees are able to adapt how they work to fit their needs and style. In turn that will make them more productive.

Eve Poole, Lecturer at Ashridge explained: "We know from executive profiling that there are real differences in preference in the management population. There is an over-representation of those who prefer logical problem-solving, for example. This contributes a usefully critical skill-set to agile working. The other key personality difference is about tolerance for uncertainty. Many managers are designed to like order and process, so agile works best for them if they can contain their anxiety about the mess in some semblance of these: micro deadlines and micro deliverables usually meet this need."

Working styles also extend to businesses. Kelly believes that often the organisation itself is ignorant what these are. "Some businesses have an underlying sub culture of presenteeism, sometimes without realising it. This is especially true if they offer their staff great perks, a fun environment to work in and believe their workplace is somewhere that their people would want to spend a lot of time in. This is common in the creative industries. However, if someone is a reflector, who thinks deeply and likes space to consider, then perhaps the buzz of the office doesn't always work for them in terms of being the best setting to get the job done. A proper agile working policy looks at what everyone is trying to achieve and how. Where they do it and within reason, the hours within which they do it, is immaterial," says Kelly, "Agile working is about celebrating different working styles and minds; these are the underpinning principles of fairness and inclusion – which is why it's often said there is a strong link between agile working and diversity."

Agile working benefits companies and individuals because it forces people to adapt quickly to a changing reality and work on a project basis. It is no longer about allocating set hours to complete tasks but instead it's about focusing on goals and outcomes, as required tasks to achieve goals can change rapidly and there's no point working through a list that won't achieve what you need it to.

Maria Eugenia Giron, a brand strategy and business development expert, explains the implications of this: "Agile working allows me to identify synergies between different projects faster than if I was working in a more traditional way. These activities do have useful synergies, and my participation in each enables me to improve with the others. However, managing them all would be a challenge if it were not for the application of agile working. You have no alternative but to adapt quickly to a changing reality. Agile working must be a fluid process. I am constantly tweaking my own management and learning as I go along."

Effective management processes and communication tools are essential but individuals also have to adapt how they manage their work. Giron advised: "To do agile working you really need to be very disciplined in your planning. You need to allocate 10% of time to changing activity so that it doesn't throw you off track. If you have a portfolio of activity, you need to dedicate time to going from one to the other."

Higham thinks that agile working particularly suits the way younger people work: "There is a link between those who work in an agile way and the entrepreneurial mindset. Research in America found that 50% of millennials describe themselves as entrepreneurial. They know they're not entrepreneurs technically but they see their role at work as focusing on their own tasks and priorities, and understanding how this links in with overall growth. The next generation in the workplace will therefore be more naturally attuned to the ways of agile working in that they want to be responsive and able to adapt in the way that entrepreneurs do."

Others believe that agile work is particularly suited to women. According to Giron "Agile working suits the way women work. We need the flexibility because we have multiple layers to our lives. In my opinion, agile working should help women break the glass ceiling, which is often very difficult in the corporate world which doesn't allow flexibility and can be caught up in politics rather than achievements. Agile working will help women achieve optimum performance."

The Office

Whether you have one person working from home, or everyone working from home, the way the 'office' is used is at the heart of agile working policies and, along with the culture of the company, it is the issue that will have the most impact on the practical implementation of an agile working policy.

What is your attitude to your office? How is it currently used: work hub, showcase for clients or an essential part of your culture? What are the risks and what are the savings? What is the impact on your reputation? For every business, the answer to these questions will be different.

Andy Hinxman, Director of Keybridge IT, has helped many companies introduce more agile working practices and he doesn't believe that remote working is right for all companies: "Working in a designated office space during designated hours works for some businesses for a number of reasons. Proximity to clients is a key reason, especially when the sector you work in may require you to visit the client site or have regular meetings. Proximity to the clients works in your favour as you can see them quickly and easily if based at a key or central site or office. Some clients prefer companies nearby to them for this very reason, and can determine which company they choose, such as an IT supplier. Some office spaces or road names can add 'prestige' or recognition to your company or the sector you work in, such as the finance industry working in Bank or Canary Wharf. In this sense, some industries are bound to space to add value to their company."

There is no doubt that some clients do want to see the offices of a business, to be reassured that it's not a 'Hustle' style operation and to see the culture of the business for themselves, but attitudes are changing rapidly. Most customers want to work with innovative, efficient businesses and agile working is an effective way of demonstrating this. Is Amazon considered less of a credible store because it does not have a high-street presence? It is therefore important to understand the attitude of clients in your sector.

In larger companies, some office presence is usually kept, even in the most agile businesses. In some sectors it is believed to be an essential part of the 'shop window' for the company. Some companies have consequently kept an office just for meetings and when people want to work together. They have benefited from huge savings in doing so. However, this has not always been successful, as many companies have found that not enough people then turned up to make the office worthwhile having. As with everything else, a policy needs to be put in place that works for the sector, the culture and the employees.

Underwood believes that having office space that can be scaled up or down is a good solution, but there is still limited understanding of how that works: "One of our clients has pioneered this approach, scaling up and down between 40-100 desks but from a permanent office space. They have truly embraced hot-desking, have re-designed the space to encourage greater collaboration and changed the way meeting rooms were being used, from places to take private calls to spaces for working together and coming up with great ideas. The important success driver for them was that the CEO and COO were completely committed and gave up their own offices to hot desk with the rest of the company. It's now working brilliantly for them, but the senior management team admitted that it took six to nine months for their teams to adjust - that's something businesses should factor into their planning and decision making."

There are now services that allow each member of your team to work from an office near them and pay by the hour. NearDesk, for example, was set up specifically to end the burden of commuting by offering offices near to people's homes on an adhoc (or regular) basis. Recognising the limitations of working from home and in coffee shops, its mission is to get everyone working one day a week near home.

If you don't have an office, there are also now a number of virtual services to give you the illusion of having one. These include virtual PAs (that answer your phone 24/7 in the name of your business and pass the messages on) and virtual office addresses (that give you the address you need, in the part of town you need, but without the expense of actually being there).

Some companies choose to work from an office because they are concerned about the security implications of remote working. Hinxman explains: "With employees working on the move the devices they use are likely to be their own, at least some of the time (mobile phones and tablets) and there is a risk that they are 'exposed' as an agile worker. Namely, they could lose their device or it could get stolen, or they might perhaps leave their device and documents open for criminals."

If you are in a sensitive sector it may be inappropriate to allow employees to discuss work in coffee shops or other public places. And even in sectors not usually sensitive, employees will need to be aware of commercial and personnel sensitivities. There are a number of software developments and training that you can use to counter these risks and it is important to have a very clear policy to ensure that sensitive data is kept safe and employees understand what is expected of them.

If this is your concern the same sensitivities apply to your employees doing any work away from the home (e.g. on mobile phones) and of course there is a risk that offices can get broken into.

What goes wrong?

There have been well-publicised cases where companies, having embraced remote working for a number of years, have moved back to a presenteeism, office based culture. Yahoo! and Bank of America both recalled people back into offices in 2013. And one of the staunchest supporters of remote working, IBM, where 40% of their employees were classified as remote workers, gave employees just 30 days in 2014 to decide whether to move to company-maintained office space (often hundreds of miles away from their homes) or leave the company. Four different reasons have been offered as explanation for this change in policy:

1. Not enough money was being saved. This is difficult to accept as it is simple mathematics that the cost of basing someone in New York (as in the case of IBM) is considerably higher than letting them work remotely. No evidence has been presented on this but other companies can show huge cost reductions.
2. More collaboration was needed. But is this worth the huge additional economic and social costs of getting people to an office every day? Couldn't the same collaboration be achieved through modern IT services and through bringing people together one or two days a week rather than every day?
3. It was a controversial way of reducing head count. Of course, these companies would not admit this but it is certainly open to question. Someone who has been working remotely for a decade or more is not going to be happy being forced back into an office environment; nor in many cases would it be practical. This makes the chance of them leaving high. However, the people who leave will be those that are most employable. I.e. Your best performing employees that other companies are always on the lookout for. The people you're left with will be those that have failed to get another job to fit their working style preferences.
4. New management doesn't understand or support remote working. A new manager without experience of remote working and with a 'command and control' mentality will naturally want to impose his or her own brand of management on a company.

Benjamin commented from his own experience of working with companies going through these changes: "The resistance to agile working mainly comes from middle managers, who struggle to accept that they can manage people they can't see. It is of course a fallacy, just because you can see someone doesn't mean they're working, and even if they are working, that they're delivering the outcomes you need. Presenteeism gives managers a false sense of security. Without it they need to find much more subtle criteria for judging employee contribution and value."

If you are going to introduce remote working, be warned, it is a controversial and morale destroying move to subsequently reverse the decision. On an emotional level, it tells your employees that you don't trust them and on a practical level they may not be able to change back. The chance of losing your best employees is very high.

Chapter 3
What is the social impact

The corporate social responsibility policies of companies are now a major influencing factor in winning clients and the ability to recruit and retain the best people[20]. Yet it is argued that the way we currently work no longer suits the needs of our society: how will a move to agile working help?

Commuting time and cost

The average daily commute for workers in Britain is one hour and 38 minutes and the average cost of commuting per month in the UK is £160, representing the equivalent of 21% of their mortgage. However, for many, the daily commute is much longer. For example, 10% in the North East of England travel longer than four hours every day.[21] This wastes time and creates a lot of stress. And the impact on the environment in terms of pollution is catastrophic (see below). Despite constant investment, our roads and public transport are overcrowded and accidents resulting in death or life changing injuries are common.

Introducing even the most limited degree of agile working would improve this situation. If, for example, everyone worked just one day from home a week, we would see a 20% reduction in road and public transport use by commuters (although of course it is not possible for everyone to work one day from home and not all traffic is commuters).

Exclusion of disabled people

Most of us will experience some degree of disability in our lifetimes, even if that is just a badly sprained ankle. And new parents discover just how challenging going anywhere with a pushchair is (and that is smaller and more manageable than a wheelchair). Those experiences should serve as a stark lesson in just how difficult it is to get around if you're not fully able. With a temporary injury, employers will often allow some degree of flexibility, perhaps allowing you to work from home rather than negotiate public transport with a crutch. But how do you manage if your disability is permanent?

The statistics are depressing:
- In the UK disabled people are nearly four times as likely to be unemployed or involuntarily out of work as non-disabled people.[22] The two most commonly stated enablers for employment among adults with impairments are modified hours or days or reduced working hours and access to transport.

---

[20] Total Immersion - BPS World https://www.bps-world.com/knowledge/totalimmersion
[21] OnePoll November 2015
[22] Department for Work and Pensions, July 2014, Family Resources Survey 2012/13, (online), available at: https://www.gov.uk/government/uploads/system/uploads/attachment_data/file/325491/familyresources-survey-statistics-2012-2013.pdf)

- The two most common barriers to work among adults with impairments are a lack of job opportunities (43%) and difficulty with transport (29%).

Employers are less likely to employ you, even if your problem is just a lack of mobility. And if you do find employment, transport challenges may force you to give it up.

This is a burden on the state, but, more importantly, robs these people of their chance to be part of society, earn their own living and keep their self-respect.

Exclusion of those with caring responsibilities

Caring for someone as little as five hours a week can have a significant impact on employment prospects, with those caring for more than ten hours a week being at marked risk of leaving the labour market altogether, costing the economy an estimated £1.3 billion.[23]

Highly-qualified mothers are also being excluded from full-time work because of a lack of flexibility in jobs. According to a study by the IPPR think-tank published at the end of 2014, two-thirds of working women were unable to vary their start or finishing times, while one in four said it was difficult to take an hour or two off work to attend to personal matters at short notice.

As our society ages, the cost of care of the elderly (and the ill or severely disabled) has become a huge burden on society and impossible for many families to afford or manage themselves. On the one hand, we applaud societies that take good care of their elderly, but on the other hand our employers make it impossible for that to be a reality in Britain. Without these carers, either the state picks up the cost or the family have to find the money to pay for a home. There have been some distressing cases where, unable to afford that cost, the elderly or infirm person has been abandoned. However, many of these people don't require constant care. Often the most important part of the care is simply being nearby should difficulties arise, so agile working is an effective way of addressing this.

Exclusion of our most experienced

Sadly, many people spend most of their working lives looking forward to retirement, but then become ill within two years of it happening. A report published in May 2013 by the London-based Institute of Economic Affairs is representative of what other studies have found. It showed that retirement increased the chances of suffering from depression by 40%, while it increased the probability of having at least one diagnosed physical ailment by about 60%.

The research[24] studied 9,000 people across 11 European Union countries and found that across borders, people suffered in the same ways and to similar degrees. Controls were used to ensure age-related conditions did not affect the result. Gabriel Sahlgren, director of research at the Centre for Market Reform of Education and author of the IEA report, was not expecting retirement to undermine health quite as much as the results showed. In the first year of retirement, health actually improved: "It's nice to get some rest from work," he explained, but within three years retirees' mental and physical health started to deteriorate. Other studies have shown similar results. And where the retirement age is different in

---

[23] Analysis from Age UK, Walking the tightrope, July 2016
[24] London-based Institute of Economic Affairs - May 2013

different countries, the results are the same. The key factor is the date of retirement, not how old the person was.

Why? There are a number of factors, including reduction in income, but the key issue is the reduction in mental and physical stimulation and the loss of the self-esteem that comes with retirement. A job gives people a sense of value and colleagues make you feel you belong, you're part of something useful. If you lose such a fundamental part of your life and sense of self-worth overnight, it should be no surprise that people deteriorate.

Agile working allows a gradual reduction in hours and responsibility whilst continuing to deliver value. It is how the most senior directors often manage their careers; who commonly move into non-executive very part-time roles as they age. If we extend similar working styles to other older people we are likely to see a sharp rise in their health.

Destruction of local communities

Mass commuting empties local communities of people during the working day, creating so-called dormitory towns and, in many places, this has killed the community spirit that is so important to well-being.

Before the industrial revolution people lived and worked together, developing solid communities made up of families and friends. We now commonly live and work in separate places and, with long commutes, it is difficult to form social relationships with those we both work and live with. Families may be scattered across the country, or even the world.

This leaves many people feeling isolated. Rates of depression and suicide have been rising at an alarming rate and is the leading cause of death among young people, particularly men. American psychologist, Thomas Joiner, developed a theory known as the interpersonal theory of suicide. The theory states that there are three main factors which can cause someone to turn to suicide. One of those is a perception that they are alone in the world and no one really cares about them[25]. For someone living in a fragmented community, perhaps not speaking to neighbours or shopkeepers from one day to the next, and working away from home, the sense that they are alone could certainly be intensified. Agile working would help return people to become part of their local communities once more. Many worry that the increase in home working will isolate people, but as it becomes more common those people will hopefully emerge out of their homes, perhaps working from a variety of coffee shops or even hot desking locations locally, to rediscover the joy of being part of the community in which they live. It is something that will need to be actively encouraged.

However, there are also economic benefits to encouraging local communities to reform. Higham explained: "Local businesses will ultimately benefit too, as restaurants and cafes will see greater footfall from those working from home or from local work hubs who would ordinarily buy their lunch from an overpriced chain in the city! There will be a wider community benefit as generally, boosting contribution to local, independent stores (especially in commuter belt towns and villages which are traditionally quiet during working hours) can have a massive impact."

---

[25] NHS Choices http://www.nhs.uk/Conditions/Suicide/Pages/Causes.aspx

Benjamin added: "The shift of consumer spend from office to local locations has the potential to economically and socially revise local communities. Even business owners want to work where they live."

Distortion of housing costs

Traditional working practices demand that people are within commuting distance of their employer every day. Employment in many countries, particularly the UK, is consequently concentrated in certain regions and around key cities. Many people are forced to move to be near these cities. House prices and rents respond to the demand by leaping disproportionately. By contrast other regions experience poverty caused by lack of employment; house prices and rents stay low as de-population shrinks the demand (unless that too is distorted by holiday home buying).

The least expensive street in England and Wales is in Sunderland, where flats are sold for an average of £14,500. By contrast a one bedroom flat in some areas in central London will typically cost around £1 million. This forces salaries to go up and for employees to suffer a low standard of living as they struggle to pay either high commute or housing costs, and usually a reluctant balance of both.

Politicians 'answer' this problem by building more and more 'affordable' homes but the only option for workers, without agile working, is for people to accept more crowded conditions. Studio flats and house-sharing well into adulthood has become accepted and normal, and the idea of having a bedroom and a front door is becoming an unachievable dream.

Employment rights

Some are concerned that the shift to agile working will also gradually erode the rights of employees. A government review of employment practices published in July 2017 summarised some of these concerns as follows[26]:

- The gig economy is used by some employers as a loop-hole for not giving employees their basic employment rights, such as minimum pay and sickness benefit, on the basis that these people are classed as self-employed. It also avoids the employer having to contribute towards national insurance payments and pensions

- The imposition of zero hours contracts, particularly where they don't allow other forms of employment, mean that the worker has no guarantee of an income which can be highly stressful

- Cash jobs, estimated to be £6bn a year, are largely untaxed

In response, some of those employers that have been criticised said it was a simple trade-off between flexibility and security. The Labour Force Survey of March 2017, for example, found that 68% of those on zero-hours contracts did not want more hours.

---

[26] The Tailor Review published July 2017 by the Government

In research published in 2017[27] the Chartered Institute of Personnel and Development (CIPD), the professional HR body, found that approximately 1.3 million people are engaged in 'gig work'. Their research also found that just 14% of workers said they did gig work because they could not find alternative employment.

However, when implemented correctly, agile working is not something that should be imposed on someone. It is *agile* to suit the needs of the employee and the employer and not one at the expense or exploitation of the other. Agile working is a way of having the freedoms of freelancing, but without the uncertainty. You can be part of the gig economy, and take different jobs and work in different places, but still have employment rights with each of those employers. It is more secure because you are not forced to rely on the income of one employer who may go bust. But you should also be able to choose not to become an employee or to flex your hours around your life.

The Government, and those with an interest and concern with this issue, need to understand this definition/approach. As things stand, there is a real risk that they will legislate against a personal choice that brings with it so many benefits to society.

Fair and available for all?

Another major criticism of agile working is that it is only an option for affluent professionals.

If you look at the people working in 'gig' economy, the socio-economic split appears quite even[28]:

- 28% of accountancy, legal advice and other consultancy work
- 18% of plumbing, building and other skilled manual work
- 17% of cleaning and other household services
- 9% of delivery or courier services

However, at the lower income levels it becomes more likely that this has been forced on them by the employer, rather than an option chosen by the employee. This is likely to be a fair reflection of what also happens with agile working. There are two reasons for this:

1. Market forces mean that lower income earners have less negotiating power (and are more likely to be exploited).

    The more saleable your skills, the higher your likely income and the more likely it is that you would have negotiated working conditions to suit your needs. I.e. To secure rare skills employers have to pay more and offer better working options. This is perhaps why agile working was first seen at board director level. To ensure it filters down to other socio-economic groups the benefits to the company have to be clear. Legislation, to avoid exploitation, may also be needed.

2. Higher paid jobs are less likely to need someone to be present to perform them (but this is not always the case).

---

[27] To Gig or Not to Gig: Stories from the modern economy – Report published by the CIPD in 2017
[28] RSA April 2017

As discussed in Chapter 2, some jobs are more suited to agile working than others and some aspects of true agile working are not options for those jobs where a key part of it is to present (you can't clean an office remotely). And these jobs tend to be those that are lower paid. However innovative employers have found that other jobs that traditionally tied people to the spot, such as call-centre worker (where toilet breaks are timed by some employers), can be delivered just as well away from the office. And of course, some well-paid jobs, such as a surgeon, surveyor or pilot, have to be present.

The other legacy issue is that flexible working has been an option only offered to mothers. This creates resentment and has put agile working into the bracket of 'benefit for some' without understanding the broader context and the benefits to employers.

There will be limits, even within companies, and there are some manageable risks, but overall agile working will see huge social benefits.

Chapter 4
What is the business impact?

Many people believe that the main arguments for agile working are social ones and connect the trend with helping more mothers return to the workforce. They see it as an additional burden and demand on businesses. However, the strongest arguments in favour of introducing more agile working come from those businesses who have made it work for their whole workforce and gained huge bottom line advantages.

Benjamin argued from his own experience: "Agile working is about the capacity to change before the case for change becomes desperately obvious. If you're not fast, you'll be last. Organisations that aren't agile will join the half of Fortune 500 companies that have disappeared since 2000."

The UK Government's report in 2009, Engaging for Success, more commonly known as the Macleod Report[29], studied organisations across the UK who had demonstrated high employee engagement and high performance. One of the key findings was that work place flexibility improves team communication and productivity. Managers who participated in the study reported improved team communication, team interaction, productivity and even customer service. In fact, 98% of managers identified no negative impact of workplace flexibility on their business.

The Global Workforce Survey conducted by Towers Watson[30] provides a detailed view into the attitudes and concerns of workers around the globe. The 2007-8 survey found that just one-fifth (21%) of employees surveyed were truly engaged in their work. Nearly four out of 10 (38%) were mostly or entirely disengaged (the last survey, in 2014 sites that four in 10 employees are now highly engaged). Profession Gary Hamel[31] responded to the 2007 survey in his book: "What Matters Now" and famously in a number of articles; "Managements' Dirty Little Secret; He said; "There are many managers who have yet to grasp the essential connection between engagement and financial success. Companies that score highly on engagement have better earnings growth and fatter margins than those that don't."

Thinking global

Many start-ups work in an agile way quite naturally, particularly where they have geographically dispersed teams. They are forced to be very lean and to find the skills they need, wherever they are. An entrepreneur is less likely to be confined by tradition as to how things should be done and is more likely to focus on solving the problem. The driver to be agile then has nothing to do with being a good employer and everything to do with economic imperative.

---

[29] Engaging for Success, a study by David MacLeod and Nita Clarke http://engageforsuccess.org/engaging-for-success
[30] The Global Workforce Survey by Towers Watson https://www.towerswatson.com/en-BM/Insights/IC-Types/Survey-Research-Results/2014/08/the-2014-global-workforce-study
[31] What Matters Now *by Prof Gary Hamel,* **Management's Dirty Little Secret**

Even kitchen table start-ups will now think nothing of trading across international borders from their first day in business. In a global economy with its different time zones and holidays, no-one can be on call to customers all the time, or they would need to work 24/7, but to an agile business it's not a problem.

Cantelo explains how overseas experts provide her company with on the ground advice on what works and what doesn't work in different countries. "A UK style press release, for example, won't suit a US audience and you need a native speaker to make sure your French press release doesn't include phrases that a French person would never use. We couldn't afford to employ these people in a traditional way, but we can in an agile way."

This rationale applies to larger businesses too. Geography is no longer the barrier it once was, because technology allows you to access the best talent, wherever you are in the world.

Agile as a business model

Some businesses have taken this one step further and set up as agile businesses from the outset, using the model to become global businesses very quickly.

Julian Stubbs is the founder and chief executive of UP THERE EVERYWHERE, which has gone from zero to sales revenue of €3 million a year. He explained: "The driver for us to establish a business in the cloud, with no employees or formal offices, were economic. The issue for many service businesses is their lack of agility and fixed overheads. UP THERE, EVERYWHERE has no employees, no offices, just people. Instead of offices we have creative spaces, where members go if and when they need."

An investor's viewpoint

According to Giron working in an agile way has synergies with how angel investors approach a project.

"We do not carry out a systematic review as such, but instead go to the end goal and ask, 'what would be the deal breakers, what would make this an impossible investment?', we do a check on those then go back to the beginning. We work like this because we need to react quickly. We often have a very short window within which to make an investment decision, and we're not the only investor in the picture. Entrepreneurs themselves are similar. They do pilots, test things, quickly learn from mistakes and adjust. There are parallels with agile working because that is about focusing on end goals and flexing the processes to achieve them."

Skills

BPS World's report, Planet Talent[32] highlighted the fact that most professional millennials now think global when searching for a job.

According to Conington, "We are going through a huge transformation in the labour market. The most developed countries in the world are trying to manage a reduction in the skilled workforce as the baby-

---

[32] Planet Talent – Published by BPS World and available to download from their website

boomers near retirement. At the same time, the global labour supply has exploded as the emerging economies really start to take off. Professionals have more choice than ever before and are choosing to work outside their native countries."

Attracting top talent from overseas presents recruiters with huge challenges, from cultural differences to immigration and employment laws. It also requires strategic vision and raises numerous practical issues. Employers need to know, for example, how to screen candidates for their ability to relocate internationally. This is significant to the UK economy as we are facing a severe skills shortage in some sectors, particularly IT and engineering, where lack of skills could stop major infrastructure projects even happening.

Conington continued: "In many cases there simply aren't enough British workers with the right skills. The media complains when large infrastructure projects are given to overseas companies, like we saw with the recent decision to award a contract to build a new nuclear power plant to China, but if we don't have the skills, we can't deliver the projects."

Another sector that is suffering skills shortages is digital and tech in the creative industries. According to the Government's own figures, the UK's creative industries are worth £84.1 billion to the UK economy. Figures published in 2016 (before the Brexit vote) showed that the sector was growing at almost twice the rate of the wider UK economy - generating £9.6million per hour. This will stall without the skills.

Business leaders have highlighted the positive impact of skilled migration; from increased innovation and trade to knowledge transfer and higher productivity. In other words, if workers themselves are agile geographically there are huge economic benefits.

But do all these jobs need people to physically migrate? The creative industries are at the forefront of agile working. Infrastructure projects will demand that some people are physically present for some of the time, but do they actually need to permanently relocate? Isn't the next step the globalisation of skills to bring in the expertise we need via the internet in agile, international teams?

Diversity

In the previous chapter we looked at the social consequences of exclusion. However, there is also an economic impact for the organisation itself.

If you look at different places of work, whether factory or office, you'll see that many organisations recruit in their own image; they recruit people who look, sound and act like them in every way (clones). Sometimes this is quite deliberate; "We only recruit our type of person/ people with a PHD," you can hear managers say with pride, but usually it is an unconscious bias. It is a comfortable thing to do, we are more relaxed with people around us who are like us.

In some instances, there is a convincing argument for sticking to a certain type of person. Restaurants and hotels, for example, will try to deliberately recruit staff who reflect their customers so that they feel at home in a familiar environment, or that reflect the ethnicity of the food they serve. However, in most cases recruiting 'clones' is bad for business. A diverse workforce has more chance of understanding a diverse customer base and will drive innovation. A 'clone' workforce will reinforce their own prejudices and stifle innovation. If they all come from the same background they are less likely to challenge and question. You are also closing off the recruitment field so are far more likely to struggle to recruit.

One of the most documented diversity issues is the lack of women going into IT and engineering, with less than 16% of female graduates in these disciplines. The statistics then get worse; just 9% of the engineering workforce are female.[33] We know that women approach technology very differently to men and have different motivations as customers. But with such a poor representation of women in these industries the future is being designed by men, for men and they commonly misunderstand the needs and motivations of women.

For years, for example, it was assumed that the number one influencing factor on a woman's choice of car was colour, but when it was researched the top factors were actually safety and fuel economy, with colour a long way down the priority list[34]. Apple also famously issued a health app that ignored women's reproductive health issues (an oversight they have since addressed).

José Neves, chief executive and founder of luxury retailer Farfetch, summed up the importance of the issue in an interview to Wired in July 2017: "Diversity isn't a moral choice - it's essential for survival. You need different points of view and different cultures, left brain and right brain, passion and technology. If everyone is looking in one direction, you'll never see what's coming up behind."

Studies have also shown that it is not just the recruitment pipeline that needs to be fixed. More than half the women who enter STEM fields leave them within a decade because of the alien culture they experience that doesn't adapt to their needs.[35]

One of the best ways of ensuring that you have a diverse workforce is to make a deliberate effort to be inclusive of different needs and different ways of working. Agile working is about celebrating different workings styles and minds; these are the underpinning principles of fairness and inclusion. It is why that it's often said there is a strong link between agile working and diversity.

---

[33] http://www.wes.org.uk/content/useful-statistics
[34] Australian study carried out in 2011 http://www.couriermail.com.au/news/forget-flashy-colours-women-want-safety-when-they-buy-a-car/news-story/69d0edbe778f098eb9f14c4415b6a674?sv=61b2f53982028f6af9ad20755d220d08
[35] Society of Women Engineers Study published in April 2016

Chapter 5
How to create an agile workforce

There is no singular framework to follow when creating an agile workforce. Richard Kauntze, chief executive of the British Council, reiterates this in a study titled What Workers Want:[36]

"It is important to remember that in creating the optimum working environment, organisations shouldn't try to adopt a one-size-fits-all approach. Rather it requires a deep understanding of the people using the space, and the work being delivered. Getting this right can be complex, but has the potential to reap considerable rewards in terms of productivity and should therefore be at the heart of any business strategy."

One of the main barriers to the success of agile working is culture and mindset, so what it requires is a shift in perceptions. Senior and middle management, for example, need to be on board with implementing change and willing to engage and empower their workforce. Once this is in place, the focus can then turn to offering flexible hours, implementing new technology or establishing whatever else has been deemed appropriate for business development.

Shifting perceptions

For a shift in perceptions to occur, senior and middle management must adopt effective communication techniques, ideally using an 'adult' approach, and not the parent/child one psychiatrist Eric Berne described in 1957 as part of his Transactional Analysis theory, which has since become a traditional management technique.

For example, seeing that Paul the programmer is agitated during a team discussion, the average line manager would normally pull him aside and say: "Paul you seem to be upset, tell me what you're feeling." This would be a nurturing parent question posed to Paul's child ego. If Paul responds, "I was feeling cut out of the conversation and I need help," he would be responding from his child state to the manager's parent.[37] This is also known as the boss-subordinate mindset.

A modern, adult approach - aka an agile mindset - involves employers being honest about business requirements and objectives and employees becoming more self-reliant without the need for micromanagement. In that order. For employees to become more self-reliant, employers must empower their workforce to feel confident about using their own initiative to innovate and drive change. Agile organisations encourage their people to do things their way. They cultivate the habit of taking risks by:

- Presenting new challenges and opportunities
- Working on identifying and developing their unique interests and abilities
- Inviting them to lead a certain task

---

[36] British Council Offices http://www.bco.org.uk/Research/Publications/What_Workers_Want_2016.aspx
[37] **Software blog** https://tcagley.wordpress.com/category/communication/transactional-analysis/

- Encouraging in-moment feedback, so that they can quickly move on to the next step
- Pushing them to think like a leader
- Creating room for independent work and decision-making[38]

Employers must also set an example. If flexible hours are recognised as the way forward, they should leave the office early themselves and work from home sometimes.

The Smart Working Code of Practice launched by the UK government in 2016 offers a guideline for managers to follow. Launched in January 2016 by BSI, the business standards company, in collaboration with the Cabinet Office, it aims to set out 'everything you need to make the Smart Working revolution work for you and your team by pulling in best practice and evidence from around the world.[39]

Restructuring workloads

While the behaviour of people is one major area of consideration, the actual structure of how work gets done is another. For a company to be truly agile, it needs to be open to multiple work models: the classic team, the ad hoc team, crowdsourcing, independent contractors, etc. You must be able to use them in various ways depending on each project, in a speedy yet effective manner. A bureaucratic hierarchy with fixed procedures just delays everything and frustrates everyone.

Shruti Malani Krishnan, co-founder of Powr of You, a consumer data and analytics hub, said: "With our team split around US, UK and India, it's all about getting the job done, and not the number of hours spent on a task or where it's spent."

Changing the workplace design can help create this multiple work model structure by placing the focus on activities instead of individuals. Hot desking, for example, merges different divisions of the company and ensures people talk to someone different every day. Collaborative spaces add to this by offering a change of scene for other sets of colleagues who need to work together on an issue and encouraging people to think beyond their primary job responsibilities and spend time coming up with new ideas.

Another way is to have a different team leader per project, as opposed to the same one each time based on seniority. A timeline and list of tangible objectives can help keep things on track while enhancing learning and everyone stays happy, secure in the knowledge they have been treated as equals.

Employees working for others

Many contracts of employment make 'moonlighting', or working for someone else at the same time, a sackable offence. Yet true agile working means allowing your employees to work for other employers.

---

[38] Laura Goodrich blog www.bkconnection.com/bkblog/laura-goodrich/how-to-build-an-agile-workforce
[39] The Smart Working Code of Practice, published 2016 https://civilservice.blog.gov.uk/2016/01/21/smart-working-the-quiet-revolution/

On the plus side, it means that you're not wholly responsible for someone's income (which appeals to conscientious start- ups and cash-poor smaller companies). It also leads to valuable cross fertilisation across the employers; a skill or connection achieved due to one employment can be very beneficial to another.

It is important to put some parameters around the work to ensure that there is no conflict of interest and that the employee doesn't take work for themselves that should come to the company. But otherwise, as alarming as some business owners find the idea, it is really no different to a freelancer working for more than one organisation at the same time. Some would argue that the employee will not be as committed or loyal. If by that you mean that you don't 'own' them or their time in the same way, that's true, but people will always be most loyal and committed to employers who treat them like a grown up and allow them to control their own lives.

Megan Knapp, a start up coach & business strategist, summarised the practical implications; "Let's be honest – almost everyone wants to see agile working catch on in a much more widespread way. Millennials take this a step further because 74% of them expect flexible schedules in the workplace. Whether it's adopted or not is up to the company; however, the implications involve the overall happiness of the workplace.

Another pro, which isn't frequently considered, is that it's a relatively inexpensive programme to implement. The technology exists, most of which is already owned (i.e. a computer, telecommuting programs, some headphones, etc.). It's not about reinventing the wheel, merely utilising existing methods. The cons are pretty obvious: perceived disconnection from the rest of the company and the need for different methods of performance and progress measurement. There will always be a negative side to a great thing. Thankfully it's easy to mitigate these opportunities."

Technology

New technology is a driving force of agile working as it allows for conference calls, shared documents and virtual collaboration. It makes it easier for people to work away from a central office but also maintains employee engagement by making them still feel part of the team.

Andy Hinxman, Director of Keybridge IT, which delivers technology services to many agile companies advises: "Each employee needs a lightweight but robust laptop for mobility. Ideally with Windows 10 Pro Operating System, 8GB RAM, a solid state drive (SSD) and an i5 core as a minimum.

"You need to ensure you have anti-virus installed, scans are run regularly, and the software is updated regularly. This is to counter cyber threats to your business.

"Cloud storage and synchronisation, such as OneDrive for Business, is also a key, to ensure that, should your device get lost or stolen, or break down, you have not lost all your work. Cloud storage and device files should be encrypted to protect the integrity of your data."

The other benefit of Cloud storage is that the whole agile team can access the same documents without the need of a server.

Meetings and teamwork

There is no doubt that meetings and teamwork can become a challenge to organise. Finding a date and time when everyone is working may not be possible, for example, so a truly agile team will flex around this and should be prepared to change their normal work plans sometimes to slot them in. For dispersed teams, it may be best to have one day in the week when they are all in the same office, or to organise quarterly off-site meetings.

But the fact that meetings aren't so straightforward to arrange can have a positive impact on productivity, as it stops 'meetings for meetings sake' and forces everyone to consider the value of the meeting before it is held.

Cantelo advised: "I've worked in organisations that are dominated by meetings, to the extent there was no time to do any real work, I spent all day running from one meeting to the next. This has a huge impact on stress levels and productivity. The cost is also huge, but people rarely consider that. The public sector is particularly bad at inviting everyone, without any thought to the cost of them being there. Now, as the owner of a remote working business, the cost, in terms of money and time, is uppermost in my mind. We carefully consider the value of each meeting before we agree to it."

For Giron there is still a role for face-to-face meetings in an agile business. "I am part of a fund of more than 100 women co-investing across Europe. We have one or two meetings per year in person as this really makes a difference to how relationships evolve, but we know that we don't need to be in one place together daily to achieve our goals. Equally, if you are working internationally, different cultures need face- to-face interactions to avoid barriers.

"If an agile business does put aside time for collaboration and meetings, it is important that this time is focused and has a strong methodology. Preparation is important, as is a good moderator and interactive technology that allows you to build and develop strategies as you talk."

Training

New recruits may require some time spent in the office before being allowed to work remotely. This way they can learn how things get done and what the company's values are in practice. Virtual companies meanwhile may need to create shadowing opportunities.

One thing critics most question is how important it is for those in a line management or mentoring role to be present, to support those they're managing.

Hinxman argues: "Managing staff can be easier when you are in the same office and you might be able to identify an issue as it arises. This is particularly key if you monitor call quality, monitor staff performance or target staff particularly. Should there be any issues, you can address them more quickly than if they were at home or on the move."

Kelly believes that these issues can be managed in many sectors: "Of course, it's great if you're learning the ropes and you want to throw a question over your shoulder to your manager. But actually there are some fantastic collaboration tools out there, like Slack, where you can do just that, from wherever you are. Naturally, when someone is new to a role, their first few weeks will require a manager to be highly present and tangible as you have to set them off on the right footing, but there's no reason for it to stay like that forever, and in fact, it can empower developing staff to become more solutions focused and confident when they feel supported from a distance but trusted to get on with it. This should be judged on a case by case basis. There will always be cases where it's best for two people to sit next to each other the majority of the time. But equally there are times and cases where technology is actually a more compelling enabler."

Top tips from Megan Knapp, start-up coach & business strategist:

- To successfully implement an agile working programme, a company must make sure everyone's on the same page and has similar benefits. People are people, and jealousy is inevitable, not to mention a tricky thing to manage. Agile working may not be applicable to every position, so how can the company account for those who won't benefit from it? Or are there ways, like incorporating flexible hours instead of remote working, for these employees?

- Then, the issue of technology has to be addressed: what else do we need before we can successfully work remotely?

- Next, create a plan for keeping company culture up even with individuals working outside of the office. This may mean more informal events, conferences, or some face-to-face meetings to keep everyone feeling connected. It has to be addressed at a company-level, as preferences will vary.

- Last, decide how progress will be monitored and performance will be reviewed. Will it still be by the hour? Will it be by the project? It's up to you as a company."

Case Study: The CAB Studios approach

CAB Studios has implemented agile working using the following five practices:

- **Flexible hours** - CAB believe that flexible working hours aren't just for people with family commitments; everyone has a personal life. Team members are able to start any time between 8-10am and don't have to ask permission, they just let their line manager know
- **Tailored jobs** - In a typical agency setup, there are often creative and client services teams, and specialists in each. CAB recognises that some people's skills span both areas and gives them opportunities in both. In some cases, their job hybridisation programme has meant one person does a job that previously took two people, by working more efficiently, drawing on creative and operational/strategic skills at once
- **Rewards** - Each CAB team member starts the month with 20 casino chips, which are used to reward colleagues who go the extra mile e.g. helping out on a project with a tight deadline or identifying times when colleagues have excelled in a presentation. At the end of each month, the person with the most chips is rewarded with a gift voucher of their choice or an extra day's

- holiday. This is in addition to a weekly celebratory 'high five', where the best examples of client work are recognised and rewarded

- **Empowerment** - Any CAB employee with a good idea is supported in making it a reality. The CAB partner programme provides those with a viable business idea that can complement the main CAB offering, with mentoring and funding support. The CAB board, for example, helps devise a business plan and bring the idea to market, acting as shareholders thereafter
- **Evolution** - While CAB is proud of its initiatives, it's always looking for ways to improve by listening to staff and supporting their needs

Testing the water

You may wish to implement aspects of agile working on a trial before committing completely. If so, consider the following:

- Are you going to implement changes across the entire company or with just one team?
- How long will you give changes before assessing impact?
- What metrics will you use to measure success?

Ultimately remember there is no set way of doing it and you are entitled to change things as you go along. 'Test and learn' is a core principle of agile working and this means letting go of at least some control and accepting that mistakes may happen along the way. The important thing is to keep the channels of communication open with your employees and respect their needs as well as being clear about your business goals.

Chapter 6
How do you measure its impact?

We have argued that agile working is a smarter approach and provided evidence of better lifestyles, with positive benefits for recruitment and retention; a reduced carbon footprint; enhanced accommodation of diversity; better mental and physical health; improved productivity; more effective use of property.[40] But if you're tasked with reporting to your board on the bottom line business benefits of introducing agile working, how do you go about measuring it?

The impact of agile working will be very different in different types of organisations. However, to test whether agile is the right course for an organisation you should look and measure the impact on the following:

- Productivity - how engaged is your workforce? Has there been an uplift in output and results?
- Costs - has it increased or decreased overhead costs? By how much?
- Recruitment - are you able to recruit and retain the right people?
- Staff development - is everyone progressing?
- Clients/customers - how are your sales going?

Productivity

In a traditional work force, whether deliberately or not, people are judged by how long they sit at their desk. Even where managers say they like to work in an 'agile fashion', those who work for them frequently express nervousness about leaving earlier than others. Even the managers themselves are reluctant to leave early for fear of 'setting a bad example'. As a result, in many organisations, someone who regularly works late will be seen as more committed than someone who leaves early. However, most managers also recognise, when challenged, that this is a misleading judgement. The last person at the office may either be very slow at their job, lack focus or waste time on social media or chatting to friends. By contrast the person who has to leave at a set time will commonly keep their head down and focus on delivering their work in the time they have.

One of the benefits of agile working is that it forces everyone, managers and staff, to measure outcomes. What is being delivered and by when? What impact does it have on the business and in reaching the business goals?

According to Nicole Lipkin, business and organisational psychologist: "An agile leader should be more interested in reaching goals rather than focusing in on the amount of hours put into reaching those goals. Additionally, an agile leader is willing to give up or take on new responsibilities in accordance with

---

[40] Civil Service blog https://civilservice.blog.gov.uk/2016/01/21/smart-working-the-quiet-revolution/

organisational needs before their own personal preferences are met. It's about the organisational goals and the collaborative success of the company."

In Spring 2017, BPS World surveyed 2,000 people (managers and employees) to rate how productive they thought part-time workers were. The experience of part-time workers and the perception of their employers did not match. The majority of employees said they thought they were more productive because they're more focused on getting the job done in the time they have, whereas the majority of employers (50.77%) think their part-time staff are more productive thanks to less distractions.   A similar proportion of employers and employees (38% and 37%) believed they were more productive because they had more energy. Employees generally felt that their part-time colleague was as productive as they were. One reason for that productivity is that part-time workers have more time away from the employer, so have more energy to devote to the work.

Perception and reality, in terms of productivity, therefore do not match and are unreliable measures. It is therefore important that SMART goals are set and agreed for everyone in the team, whether they are agile workers or not, and that the productivity of individuals is based on these goals

Of course, there are issues outside of work goals that can affect this productivity. One of the key issues will be communication. If one member of the team has to wait for another to be available that can hold a project up. Lack of 'water-cooler' moments meanwhile keep some in the dark on key issues that affect them. When measuring productivity, the impact on communication should therefore be considered and if issues are identified, a costed strategy for overcoming them needs to be implemented.

There are legitimate concerns that some aspects of agile working - if managed badly - could increase stress levels. Professor Gail Kinman, an occupational health psychologist at the University of Bedfordshire and the British Psychological Association, believes that there is an increasing problem of people "grazing" their work; checking e-mails and taking calls outside of office hours. Research shows that each time they then performed a work task, their stress levels went back up.

Kinman explained: "If you keep picking at work, worrying about it, your systems never really go down to baseline so you don't recover properly. You might sleep, but you don't sleep properly, the effectiveness of your immune system reduces."

When this research was reported in the Guardian it was cited as evidence that flexible working is bad for your health. But what is being described is how we're now all working, whether we're office-based or not. It is not peculiar to aspects of agile working, but it does point to the need for clear policies to manage and reduce the "always on call' mentality that we now have.

Case study – Ctrip in China

Nicholas Bloom, a Stanford Graduate School of Business professor, tested his belief that working from home improved well-being of employees by studying China's largest travel agency Ctrip, which has 20,000 employees. The company's initial drive to offer remote working was to reduce overheads. They used volunteers for the study and a control group. Half worked from home for nine months, coming into the office one day a week, and the other half worked only from the office. The two groups were tracked for two years.

The results were impressive and conclusive: "We found a 13% improvement in performance from people working at home," Prof Bloom reported.

He cited two reasons for this: first, people working from home clock in a full day. Those in the office experience transport delays, chats with colleagues, long lunches and leave early to fulfil domestic needs. Second, people at home concentrate better. "The office is actually an amazingly noisy environment. There's a cake in the break room; Bob's leaving, come join. The World Cup sweepstakes is going. Whatever it is, the office is super-distracting," he said.

Among those employees allowed to work from home, resignations at the company dropped by 50%. Not only did the employees benefit, the managers did too because they spent less time painfully advertising, recruiting, training, and promoting.

The experiment led Ctrip to offer a work-from-home option to all its employees. The company reported that it made US$2,000 more per person for every home worker.

Costs

One of the key drivers for many businesses to introduce agile working is cost reduction. Start-up companies may not be able to afford an office, or to employ the skills they need full-time. Larger companies and public sector organisations may needs to reduce their overheads. Key costs to consider are below. Some are very tangible and easy to measure, others can be hidden. Some are additional costs, some represent huge savings.

1. Office or shop – with rents and business rates ever on the increase having a small premise, or being wholly virtual (or online), creates huge savings for the business.

2. IT system – to facilitate agile working, most organisations will need a reliable, secure but easy to access cloud-based system. These are not expensive and are recommended for office-based businesses too so should not usually be counted as an additional cost unless the introduction of agile working requires a move away from server-based system. However, there may be additional IT support costs. For example, you may need to supply printers for home use.

3. Training, ideas and partnerships - an agile worker who brings in ideas, experience and connections from their other work could reduce the need for training and speed projects up. The benefits to productivity can be considerable, but won't be easy to measure. Instead qualitative questions have to be asked, such as:

- Did we gain additional skills that the company didn't have to pay for?
- Were any key partnerships forged that would not have happened without agile working?
- What financial benefit did the company gain from them?

The Flex Factor report by the RSA (Royal Society for the encouragement of Arts, Manufactures and Commerce), for example, surveyed 2,828 workers and found that companies could save £650 per annum/per employee on desk space. This could gain £6.9bn productive hours, nationally; along with £1.1bn in workstation costs.[41]

Recruitment

The best people have their pick of employers as the best employees are the key to the success of most businesses. Anything that makes it easier to recruit those people will therefore have a positive impact on the business.

In the BPS Survey 44.6% of employees said that they would be more likely to work for a company that offered agile working, only 5% said they would be less likely.

Due to the social issues, detailed in other chapters, offering agile working will open up access to employees who would not otherwise consider working for you.

"This way of working is being introduced by many businesses as a USP and works well in attraction strategies" explained Conington. "We speak with organisations who are starting to embrace agile working and others that are still more traditional, yet the common theme is their ambition to harness the strongest talent. This talent knows their worth and can demand levels of flexibility. It will no longer be a USP to offer agile working, it is swiftly becoming a necessity."

Agile working and the offer of more flexibility in the workplace has dramatically altered the retention rates at BPS World. They now enjoy an unprecedented 92% retention rate, attributed to a combination of factors, but in part due to a less structured workplace environment and greater levels of flexibility.

This has led to further, perhaps unexpected, benefits. Pride in their brand and culture has increased, they have more loyalty which has had a direct impact on the need to hire. It has also encouraged greater levels of collaboration and creativity from some unlikely sources.

"Our workplace environment had to adapt and change to suit the flexible and agile nature of our business. We actively encourage people to work remotely when possible and promote a hot desking approach in our office. This fosters greater understanding of each other's roles and reduces the silo effect often experienced in organisations. As a healthy by-product, individuals also produce less clutter (hence waste) as they are more mindful of others and the space they leave".

Staff development

In a traditional way of working, junior employees work alongside more senior employees and the majority of their professional development happens informally, as they work, listening in and seeing how others manage things. Agile working can reduce that vital informal training (as discussed earlier).

SMART training plans become even more important and, where the employee has little contact with other team members, innovative ways need to be found to ensure that development happens. Organisations should ask:

---

[41] RSA https://www.thersa.org/discover/publications-and-articles/reports/the-flex-factor

- What informal development takes place for office based employees?
- How important is it for the business and for the individual? Are there key members of the team who are particularly good at coaching others?
- What impact has agile working had on that training?

Stubbs commented: "Our cloud based tools include FaceTime, Skype and Go TO Meeting – which allow screen sharing / file sharing and video conferencing. We invest in training sessions and meet ups - and every so often just a party! We have found engagement and interaction improves tremendously with really getting to know people."

However agile working itself can develop staff faster and more effectively, particularly for leadership roles.

Poole explained why: "The process [of agile working] requires them to trust their instincts more - and trust others - and to try things. While sometimes things fall by the wayside, the opportunities that rapid iteration presents for small failures as well as small triumphs mean that mistakes are easily absorbed, but the steady drip of the feedback loop builds confidence over time. I don't have the evidence to support this, but my impression is that both the speed and quality of participation improves from project to project, so there is a compounding effect that acts as a ratchet on the quality of agile outcomes over time. For aspiring leaders, agile working offers an important masterclass is ambiguity, accountability and partnerships - all crucial leadership practices for the future."

Customers

Where a business is young and/or small and where it has introduced agile working solely to save costs, there can be a temptation to present a more traditional 'shop window' to customers and clients. This is understandable, many clients will be reassured by seeing the office of the business, the traditional office is more tangible and it is a chance to soak up the atmosphere. The benefits and risks therefore need to be carefully weighed but being open about the nature of the working practices is recommended.

Businesses should ask:
- What has been the reaction of clients/customers? Have sales gone up or have they been more difficult to close? Can it be attributed to the change?
- If negative, how is the change presented to customers? E.g. In a service business, can the cost savings be shown to give better value to customers?
- If positive, why? Has it helped present the company as more forward thinking? Is it matching the way the clients are now working? How can the company build on that positivity?

Chapter 7
What is the future of agile working?

The evidence is clear and experts agree, agile working is here to stay and set to become more commonplace.

Malani Krishnan doesn't think we can go back from where we are now: "The original idea of a prototypical office existed because the coordination costs were much higher when people weren't together. With the number of tools out there, this is no longer the case. Flexible working is only going to be on the rise, and employees will work as and when and where they want, with the job being what's important and not physical proximity to a water cooler."

According to Working Anywhere: A Winning Formula for Good Work by Lancaster University's Work Foundation, 70% of organisations will have some form of flexibility in place by 2020. Dr Cathy Garner, director of The Work Foundation and author of the report, said: "The evidence is showing a clear trend towards a more flexible way of working in the UK as the hurdles are overcome by fresh innovations in technology and people management. We believe that employees and their employers will benefit from the 'virtuous circle' created, whereby improved job design, work organisation and trusting relationships lead to healthier, happier and more productive workplaces."[42]

So, it is clear that agile working has now become a mainstream concept that no organisation can afford to ignore but what will this mean?

The Economy

A study by Citrix and Centre for Economics and Business Research at the end of 2014[43] estimated that increased flexible, 'work from anywhere' culture could add £11.5 billion annually to the UK economy.

£7.1 billion came from reduced commuting costs, and the estimated over half a billion hours spent travelling. The study also found that flexible working cultures can result in the economically inactive or unemployed returning to work and, potentially, boosting GDP by up to 4.7%

Historically, the UK has struggled with overall productivity rates compared to other nations. An analysis of global GDP rates carried out last year by the Organisation for Economic Cooperation and Development (OECD) found the UK languishing at number 16, with Luxembourg ranking top. The same study also identified that a seven-hour working day is best for optimum productivity, yet the average working day for Britons is 8.5 hours, with many working much longer hours.

---

[42] Citrix https://www.citrix.com/content/dam/citrix/en_us/documents/
[43] https://cebr.com/reports/impacts-of-a-flexible-working-culture/

Recruitment

The most employable expect flexibility in many sectors and will shun those employers who don't offer it. Flexibility is now a far greater driver and influencer when it comes to job hunting, than it was a few years ago. In the last decade, there's been a shift from people focused on job security and salary to more broader considerations like flexibility and development opportunities. It means that those companies who embrace agile working will be first in line when it comes to attracting the best talent. And if they attract the best talent you can be sure that they will be the high growth, successful companies of the future.

When you're no longer tied to one location it is possible for a business to embrace the global economy without. BPS World's report; Planet Talent, found that millennials will look globally for jobs, with the rise of agile working they will be able to do that without leaving home.

The Office

Offices are not likely to die out completely but they are expected to significantly change, and these changes can be seen already.

According to the British Council for Offices, the UK spent an estimated £28.5 billion on offices in 2012, making it by far the biggest expense after staff. Despite this dominance in the annual accounts of most organisations, nearly three fifths (57 per cent) of 250 senior executives from large organisations in a poll carried out by the Centre for Economics and Business Research (Cebr) and Populus) do not discuss property in the boardroom regularly. The rise of agile working is changing this. The benefits of an office will have to be justified against the cost, it cannot be assumed as an essential business need.

The public sector has recognised that agile working can reduce the cost of its property and, since 2010, has sold off £1 billion of what it considers underutilised space and is encouraging departments to share offices. Similar initiatives are happening at local level. This could be taken one step further with officials from different government departments being actively encouraged to use official office space nearer to where they live (as they already are at times of severe transport or weather problems).

However, some people don't want to work at home alone, they want to work with others or they find it very difficult to work alone. But even in this group most don't want to go into an office *every day*. This is likely to lead to a boom in the creation of workspaces as social environments, especially in residential areas. We're already seeing the start of this boom but, at the moment, many of these people still go to coffee shops just to get out of the home environment.

We are also likely to see many more mixed-use buildings. For example, Staples in the USA had a big issue with retail footprint. They owned thousands of square feet in terms of retail space, but didn't need it, as people increasingly bought online. Consequently, they started renting out the excess space to businesses on a flexible basis.

Housing

Freed from the need to be within daily commuting distance from their place of work we can expect the population to start to spread out more, with a consequent impact on housing costs (it will reduce in cities and increase in desirable but less connected areas).

Infrastructure

Between 2013 and 2030, the total cumulative cost of congestion to the UK economy has been estimated to be £307 billion.[44]

The research found that nearly 70% of the UK workforce commuted to work by car during peak times, with the average British driver spending 124 hours stuck in gridlock annually, and, assuming there are no major changes to the way we work, this is set to rise to 136 hours in 2030, equivalent to 18 working days a year.

There is an obvious cost to the driver in terms of fuel and wasted time that could have been spent productively working nearer home. However, the gridlock also increases the cost of deliveries, which has to be passed onto consumers.

The government is continually having to spend out eye-watering sums to improve our road and public transport networks to take ever increasing numbers of passengers. High Speed 2 (HS2) alone has a projected cost of £56 billion.

Major infrastructure projects do also have a positive effect on the economy, particularly in terms of employment. However, if congestion decreased because a few more people started to work from home, just one day a week, money could instead be spent on infrastructure projects that improve our quality of life, such as hospitals and schools.

We have to ask ourselves - do employers really need 70% of the population to attend their place of work EVERY day. Is the cost really worth it?

Stubbs highlights the absurdity of the current way of working in an interview to the Journal of Advertising Research: "I have been in marketing consultancy for 20 years. For most of that time I have spent at least three hours a day in a car, commuting about 70 miles a day, to and from work, where 50 other people had made similar journeys to the office by one mode of transport or another. All had consumed energy in some form, pumped out CO_2 and wasted a fair amount of time and effort in doing so. On a typical day I would truly interact with no more than four or five people, and even fewer on some days, then I would have to face the commute back again, to arrive home late, tired and not particularly happy."

---

[44] INRIX and the Centre for Economics and Business Research published October 2014

Public Policy

The shift to agile working has numerous game-changing impacts on what we need from government and the public sector that warrant a number of in-depth studies of their own, but with a few exceptions the enormous potential of agile working has not been appreciated.

Benjamin, for example, has tried to highlight the transport issue: "The Government and organisations, such as Transport for London, are spending billions of pounds on improving transport capacity. The suggestion of instead funding employers to increase home and near home working has been dismissed as a fantasy."

Many agile workers are struggling with a tax and benefit system that only recognises traditional employment and penalises those who wish to work differently. Qdos Contractor CEO, Seb Maley, said: "Recent changes to IR35 in the public sector in particular has reduced one of the benefits of freelancing and contracting. It's in the best interests of the Government to build a tax system which allows freelancers and contractors to flourish and continue working this way, rather than making their lives more complicated."

The Global Picture

There is consensus, in numerous studies, that flexible working, moving to full agile working, is growing as a way of managing work across the globe. Virgin Media Business[45], for example, have predicted that globally, 60% of office-based employees will regularly work from home by 2022.

In the 11th Annual State of Agile report[46] the top three global reasons for companies introducing agile working were all connected to improving the business:

1. Accelerate product delivery
2. Enhance ability to manage changing priorities
3. Increase productivity

This will continue to be driven by improvements in technology and is likely to be further transformed by AI, which many believe will transform our working lives as much as electricity did before it[47]. One thing that unites us globally is the importance of smartphones. In some countries where fixed line broadband hasn't been available (parts of central America and Africa), a smartphone gives people proper access to the internet for the first time. The use of smartphones, a fundamental tool for living and working, is spanning continents, and using devices to work from wherever you are, without time boundaries, has global appeal.

---

[45] Virgin Media carried out by Polycom and published in 2015
[46] 11th Annual State of Agile Report, produced and published by VersionOne 2017
https://explore.versionone.com/state-of-agile
[47] The McKinsey Global Institute – The evolution of employment and skills in the age of AI
http://www.mckinsey.com/global-themes/future-of-organizations-and-work/the-evolution-of-employment-and-skills-in-the-age-of-ai

According to Higham: "There may be a boom in agile working in parts of Asia as the rate of start-ups is growing phenomenally, and many of them will naturally start off as agile. This is true of many Silicon Valley start-ups; a huge proportion of these businesses were formed by people who didn't fit into the nine to five way of working and wanted to challenge the status quo in some way. These people didn't want to conform and they want to design work around their life and around priorities. This disruptive approach has generated many high-profile success stories."

There are of course different challenges and drivers in different countries towards agile working. Some of these are summarised below.

China

The study by Virgin Media Business claimed that China is leading the world in allowing and enabling staff to work from any location, on any device (69%).

Severe problems with air quality, the cost of offices and congestion have meant that foreign firms have led the way in offering flexible working arrangements to white collar employees. These do not appear to extend to full agile working and tend to be limited to flexible start and finish times and telecommuting. There is evidence, however, that a small but growing number of employers are looking at more creative arrangements.[48]

US

There are no legislated rights to agile, or even flexible working. Instead flexible working arrangements are negotiated based on the individual facts so no two are the same. Despite this the study by Virgin Media put them second (at 63%) of countries in allowing and enabling staff to work from any location, on any device.

The Alfred P. Sloan Foundation's Workplace, Work Force, and Working Families Program found that nearly 80% of US employees want more flexibility and has set itself the goal of promoting agile working as the "default working practice in the US".

The US Shriver Report[49] cited flexibility as one of the critical workplace solutions for keeping both women and men engaged and thriving at work.

Employers who do move towards more agile working tend to do so as a way of keeping high performing female employees or to meet their disability legal requirements.

---

[48] Survey by US China Business Council 2014

[49] The Shriver Report - A Woman's Nation Pushes Back from The Brink published in 2014 in the USA

http://shriverreport.org/special-report/a-womans-nation-pushes-back-from-the-brink/

Europe

In Europe, on average three out of four employees have some work-schedule flexibility, and this rises to 9 in 10 employees in the Netherlands and Nordic countries[50] but is just 50% in Greece.

France

The French are more passionate than most nations about the importance of maintaining a good work-life balance and it is even recognised in law. However more recently the Government has been looking at how increased flexibility can help employers reduce costs, such as overtime.

However, things are complicated in France with business licence requirements in some areas which require some form of registration for employees working from home.

Germany

Germany has seen a growth in agile working and has a number of laws related to employers offering flexible working models.

In some circumstances (related to size of employer and time spent at the company) employees can request a reduction in hours, but the employer can deny the request.

Many of the larger organisations offer a variety of agile working options, these are regulated by collective agreements and have to be agreed between employee and employer.

Netherlands

9 out of 10 employees benefit from some degree of agile working. The Working Hours Adjustment Act in the Netherlands, gives workers in companies with at least 10 employees, the right to choose their working hours. Employers have to consent to employee requests unless they can provide compelling management or business reasons to deny the request.

Employees also have the right to request a change to working times and workplace. The employer can refuse the request to remote working but they can only refuse the request for changing working times if they can demonstrate a compelling business case.

Italy

Increased agile working is being introduced as a way of tackling high unemployment and making the job market more dynamic.

Similar to the UK, there have been legal requirements for flexible working for some time, but that usually applies to part-time working.

A Final Word

Benjamin summarised the potential of agile working; "The pay back of increased agile working to the UK economy, business productivity, the environment, society and the health and well-being of people is so

---

[50] Be Flexible! Background brief on how workplace flexibility can help European employees to balance work and family. Published September 2016 by OECD

dramatic that it should be given far greater priority by policy makers. We should, for example, be looking at how we encourage house builders to include home working space in every new build in the same way indoor toilets and bathrooms are a given."

Conington explained the skills imperative behind agile working; "We are already experiencing the economic impact of a severe shortage of people at all skills levels. Employers are no longer in the driving seat; they have to work hard to attract and retain the people they need. There is a major hotel chain in London, for example, who have had to close 10% of their rooms as they cannot recruit the staff they need to service them. At the other end of the scale, major UK engineering projects, such as Hinckley Point, are having to be given to overseas contractors (to howls from the media) but if we don't have the right skills we're not in a position to deliver these projects. Offering agile working immediately increases the size of the talent pool employers can fish in and makes you more attractive to potential employees. It is not for everyone, or all businesses, but this won't go away, you can either lead the way, and win some great recruits, or you can get dragged along and perhaps have to close 10% or more of your business."

Generation X author Douglas Coupland is even more passionate. "The nine to five is barbaric. I really believe that. I think one day we will look back at nine-to-five employment in a similar way to how we see child labour in the 19th century," he said in an interview with The Guardian.[51] "The future will not have the nine till five. Instead, the whole day will be interspersed with other parts of your life. Scheduling will become freeform."

Authors and Contributors

Authors

Anne Cantelo, MD of Onyx
Charlotte Clarke, former Financial Times Journalist

We are grateful to all our contributors for their time (in order of their inclusion):

William Higham, futurologist and founder of NextBigThing

Simon Conington, Managing Director and Founder of BPS World

Amanda Underwood, Group HR Director at WSH, the parent company for well-known restaurant brands including Benugo and Searcy's

Kirstie Kelly, Executive HR Director at CAB Studios and Head of Diversity and Inclusion at Capita

Eve Poole, lecturer at Ashridge Business School

Maria Eugenia Giron, a brand strategy and business development expert

Andy Hinxman, Director of Keybridge IT

Léon Benjamin, a collaboration practitioner and co-founder of Sei Mani

Julian Stubbs, the founder and chief executive of UP THERE EVERYWHERE

Megan Knapp, a start-up coach & business strategist

Nicole Lipkin, business and organisational psychologist

About BPS World

BPS World are global total talent management experts who work across a number of sectors. They were founded by Managing Director Simon Conington in 2001. In 2016 BPS World were awarded #19 in EMEA by LinkedIn in their Top 25 Most Socially Engaged Recruitment Company List. In 2016 BPS World were also named in the Top 500 Recruitment Companies.

BPS World were also named in the Recruitment International Top 250 report 2014-16, placing them in the top 2% of recruitment companies in the UK. They were also cited as one of LinkedIn's Top 25 Inspiring Companies and nominated by REC (Recruitment Employment Confederation) in 2013, 2014, 2015 and 2016 as Best Company to Work For, Best Apprentice of the Year in 2015 and won in 2016, and Best Business Manager of the Year for 2016.

https://www.bps-world.com/total-talent-management

About Onyx Media and Communications

Onyx is a business communications consultancy working across the UK and in the US to deliver brand review, reputation management, media relations and content. They have experience working for international brands, primarily in B2B sectors such as technology, business services and banking.

https://onyxcomms.com/

Printed in Poland
by Amazon Fulfillment
Poland Sp. z o.o., Wrocław